Food and Recipes of the Native Americans

George Erdosh

The Rosen Publishing Group's
PowerKids Press™
New York

The recipes in this cookbook are intended for a child to make together with an adult.

Many thanks to Ruth Rosen and her test kitchen.

Published in 1997 by The Rosen Publishing Group, Inc.
29 East 21st Street, New York, NY 10010

First Edition

Book Design: Danielle Primiceri

Photo Credits: Cover (left) © Bettmann, (right) © Julian Cotton/International Stock; p. 4 © Joe Viesti/Viesti Associates, Inc.; p. 7, 12 (top), 20 © Bettmann; pp. 18 (top, middle) © Morgan Williams/Viesti Associates, Inc.; p. 8 (top) © W. P. Fleming/Viesti Associates, Inc.; p. 8 (middle) © Ron Rovtar/FPG International; p. 11 © UPI/Corbis-Bettmann; pp. 12 (middle), 14, 16 (top) © Corbis-Bettmann; p. 16 (middle) © Photo Shot/Bavaria/Viesti Associates, Inc.; p. 20 (middle) © Joe Viesti/Viesti Associates, Inc.

Photo Illustrations: pp. 8 (middle, bottom), 12 (middle, bottom), 16 (bottom), 18 (middle, bottom), 20 (middle, bottom); pp. 9, 13, 17, 19, 21 by Christine Innamorato and Olga Vega.

Erdosh, George, 1935–
   Food and recipes of the Native Americans / George Erdosh.
       p.   cm. — (Cooking throughout American history)
   Includes index.
   Summary: Describes the different kinds of food and methods of cooking that had been common to Indians in each of five areas of the United States. Includes recipes.
   ISBN 0-8239-5116-2
   1. Indians of North America—Food—Juvenile literature. 2. Indian cookery—Juvenile literature. [1. Indians of North America—Food. 2. Indian cookery.] I. Title. II. Series.
E98.F7E73 1997
641.59'297—dc21
                                                     97-11910
                                                         CIP
                                                         AC

Manufactured in the United States of America

Contents

Food and the Native Americans

Nancy was eating a hot dog and some potato chips when she first thought about food and the Native American Indians. Nancy was a nine-year-old Seminole Indian girl. She lived on a Seminole **reservation** (reh-zer-VAY-shun) in Florida. Nancy wondered what Indians ate before European **settlers** (SET-ul-erz) brought new foods to North America. Did they eat hamburgers, pancakes, and ice cream, just like she did?

Nancy and her family decided to take a trip across the country to answer Nancy's question about what Native Americans ate long ago. They visited Native American tribes all over the United States. Nancy spent time with some of the oldest people in the tribes. She thought they would know the most about the **traditional** (truh-DISH-un-ul) foods of their tribe.

◀ *The traditional foods of Native Americans are much different from the foods that most Native Americans eat today.*

Many Tribes, Many Foods

Nancy learned that there were many Native American tribes in North America. Each tribe ate different kinds of food. The food was often very different from what Native Americans eat today.

All Native American tribes ate the plants, berries, fruits, and vegetables that grew on their homeland. Some tribes grew their own food on farms. Others gathered these foods from the land. Most tribes hunted for meat too.

Nearly all Native American tribes grew corn. Corn was considered very important, or **sacred** (SAY-kred). A good crop of corn meant that everyone would have food through the winter.

Nancy also learned that there were five major areas in what is now the United States in which the Native Americans once lived: the Southwest, the Pacific Coast, the Plains, the Northeast, and the South.

Many Native American tribes, such as the Sioux, hunted buffalo for meat, fur, and skins. ▶

The Southwest Deserts

The Southwest has many deserts and little rain. The Indian tribes of the deserts, such as the Pueblo, Zuni, and Hopi, grew corn, beans, chili peppers, squash, and melons. Because food was sometimes hard to grow or find, it was highly respected by these tribes. To prepare for times when there was little food, Southwestern Indians stored food, such as corn and beans. They also hunted rabbits and other animals. To prepare for winter, Southwestern tribes collected the seeds of wild grasses and boiled the juice of cactus fruits to make sweet syrup and jam.

Many kinds of corn were grown in the Southwestern deserts. The Hopi Indians grew many different kinds of corn. Yellow corn, which is the sweetest corn, was used for roasting and eating off the cob. White corn was ground and used to make cornmeal mush or cornmeal bread. Red and blue corn were also ground, but they were baked into breads or pastries.

Indian Fry-Bread

You will need:

2 cups flour

1 teaspoon baking powder

½ teaspoon salt

warm water

¼ cup vegetable oil

The Native Americans made fry-bread from corn flour. Because corn flour is now hard to find, we'll make it from wheat flour.

HOW TO DO IT:

☞ Sift together the flour, baking powder, and salt into a bowl.

☞ Slowly add warm water while stirring. Keep adding water until you have a dough that feels like mud.

☞ Mix and knead the dough with your hand until it is smooth. If the dough is sticky, sprinkle with flour.

☞ Cover the dough with a towel and let it rest for 10 minutes.

☞ Break the dough into lemon-size pieces. Roll each piece into a ball and flatten into a pancake.

☞ Heat the oil in a heavy frying pan. Add as many pieces of bread as will fit in the pan.

☞ Fry the pieces on each side until they are brown.

☞ Take the brown fry-breads out of the oil and place them on a plate covered with a paper towel.

☞ Serve the fry-breads with salt, or with maple syrup.

This serves about four people.

The Pacific Coast

The people on the Pacific Coast had plenty of food, including fish, shellfish, many wild plants, berries, nuts, and mushrooms. There were also many wild animals in the forests that they could hunt.

The Native Americans of the Pacific Coast also fished for their food. One kind of fish, called salmon, is plentiful in the rivers of that area. The Indians, such as the Kwakiutl, Sokomish, and Quileute, cooked their fish over hot coals, as many people do today on a barbeque grill. They also ate shellfish, such as clams and mussels, which they steamed on heated rocks.

The Indians usually caught more fish than they could eat. They smoked the extra fish to keep it from spoiling. They stored this smoked fish to eat during the winter.

One traditional Native American way to fish is by using a spear. ▶

The Plains

Meat was the main food of the **Plains** (PLAYNZ) Indians. The plains are in what is now the midwestern part of the United States. Many Plains Indians, such as the Sioux, Chinook, and Crow, hunted and ate buffalo. Huge buffalo herds grazed the plains. The Plains Indian tribes followed the buffalo. They killed only as many buffalo as they could use. They ate the buffalo meat and used the **hides** (HYDZ) for clothing and shelter.

When it was hard to find buffalo, the Plains Indians hunted deer and rabbits. They also gathered wild rice, seeds, and plants.

Some tribes, such as the Mandan, did not move with the buffalo. They settled in one area and farmed the land. Their crops included corn, pumpkin, squash, and beans.

Pumpkin-Corn Sauce

You will need:

1 15-ounce can
   plain pumpkin
   (without spices)
1 cup canned or
   frozen corn
½ teaspoon salt
2 tablespoons
   honey

HOW TO DO IT:

☞ Preheat the oven to 350° F. Grease a baking sheet with a small amount of oil.

☞ Put the corn on the oiled baking sheet and bake for 20 minutes.

☞ Mix the corn, pumpkin, salt, and honey in a medium-size pot.

☞ Heat it over medium heat until it starts to bubble.

☞ Turn the heat to low and cook for 10 minutes, stirring from time to time.

☞ Serve with grilled chicken or pork.

This serves about four people.

The Northeast

Some tribes of the northeastern area of what is now the United States include the Iroquois, Oneida, and Algonquin. Usually it was easy for these tribes to find food, especially along the seashore, where fish and shellfish were caught. The forests had many wild animals that were hunted. These tribes also gathered wild berries and fruits. Some of them tapped maple trees for sap, which could be made into maple syrup.

Many of the tribes in the Northeast were excellent farmers. They grew corn, beans, pumpkins, and squash. The Native Americans knew that it was important to **fertilize** (FER-til-yz) the soil. Because of this, they were able to farm on the same area of land for many years.

Native American farmers knew how to grow crops so that the soil remained fertile for many years.

The South

Native American tribes in the South, such as the Seminole, Cherokee, Chickasaw, and Creek, had a good climate for growing crops such as corn, sweet potatoes, and peanuts. Hickory nuts were another important crop. Many tribes boiled the hickory nuts, squeezed the oil from them, and made a kind of milk that could be used in cooking. They also dried the nuts and ground them into nut flour, which was used to thicken soups and to make bread.

The Indians in this area also ate meat and fish. They cooked them in thick stews.

Baked Sweet Potato

You will need:

4 medium-size
sweet potatoes

HOW TO DO IT:

☞ Preheat the oven to 400° F.

☞ Scrub the sweet potatoes well under water. Poke them several times with a fork.

☞ Cover a small baking sheet with aluminum foil. Put the sweet potatoes on the foil and put the pan in the oven.

☞ Bake the sweet potatoes for one hour.

☞ Take them out of the oven and serve.

☞ Serve with butter, a sprinkle of brown sugar, or maple syrup.

This serves four people.

Native American tribes of the South used sweet potatoes in many dishes. But one of the easiest and best-tasting ways to eat sweet potatoes is baked.

Cooking and Baking

Most Native American tribes roasted their meat over an open fire. But the Southwestern and Southern Indians liked stews, which they cooked in clay pots. Indian women also baked meat and vegetables in clay pots that they buried in the ground with hot coals. A few hours later, they dug up the pots and the family meal was ready.

Some tribes liked to cook their food in clay pots that had small holes in them. Hot steam flowed through the holes to cook the food.

Some Southwestern Native Americans built large beehive-shaped clay ovens called **hornos** (OR-nohz). An *horno* was used to bake cornbread and cook stews.

Indian Vegetable Mush

You will need:

2 cups canned corn

1 medium-size zucchini, chopped

1 green pepper, chopped

2 tablespoons sunflower seeds

½ teaspoon salt

½ cup water

HOW TO DO IT:

☞ Put all of the ingredients into a blender or food processor.

☞ Add ½ cup water.

☞ Turn the machine on and off until it cuts the vegetables into tiny pieces and then mashes them. You may need to add a little more water to help the machine with the mashing.

☞ Pour the vegetable mixture into a pot and heat over medium heat. Stir every once in a while.

☞ When the mixture starts to bubble, turn the heat down low and cook for ten minutes.

☞ Stir often.

This serves two people.

To make this recipe, Southwestern Native American women mashed their vegetables in a shallow, bowl-shaped rock, called a metate. We will use a blender or a food processor.

Travel Food

While at home, most Native Americans ate only one big meal a day. But many Indians had to travel for days to hunt or fish. For these trips, Indian women prepared special food. These foods were **nutritious** (new-TRISH-us), easy to carry, and did not spoil.

One such food was called pemmicam, or dried meat cakes. Another was Indian jerky, which was dried meat. Indian jerky often was made of buffalo meat. Some Indians carried a mixture of fine corn flour and sweet syrup to eat with the meat. Others carried a mix of dried berries and turnips.

On her trip, Nancy didn't taste any of these traditional travel foods. Like most Native Americans today, Nancy and her family stopped at restaurants while they were traveling.

Pinole

½ cup yellow
cornmeal
2 tablespoons
honey
½ teaspoon
cinnamon
1 cup boiling water

HOW TO DO IT:

☞ Heat a heavy frying pan on medium-high heat.

☞ When the pan is hot, sprinkle in the cornmeal to dry roast it.

☞ Stir until you see the cornmeal starting to turn brown. This will take about six to eight minutes. Keep stirring the cornmeal or else it will burn.

☞ When it's brown, scrape the cornmeal into a small bowl.

☞ Add the honey and cinnamon and mix well.

☞ Stir one tablespoon of this mix into 1 cup of boiling water, as the Native Americans did, and let it sit for ten minutes.

This serves one person.

Pinole is a sweet, hot drink the Southwestern Indians made with blue cornmeal. They used wild herbs for flavoring, but we'll use cinnamon. Blue cornmeal is not easy to find, but you can use regular yellow cornmeal.

Sharing Is the Rule

Nancy learned a lot on her trip. She learned that long ago, Native Americans did not eat hamburgers, pancakes, or ice cream. However, they did eat buffalo meat, fry-bread, and pinole.

But one of the most important things Nancy learned was that food was sacred to Native Americans. They were careful not to waste any of it. The Indians believed that food must be shared with others. They also believed that food should not be eaten alone. Families ate the main meal of the day together. Meals were also the center of many celebrations. And some feasts lasted for several days. Food was a gift from the earth. And the Native Americans were thankful for this gift.

Glossary

fertilize (FER-til-yz) To make soil rich for growing many crops.

hide (HYD) The skin of an animal.

horno (OR-noh) Beehive-shaped clay oven created and used by some Native Americans in the Southwest.

nutritious (new-TRISH-us) Containing anything that a living thing needs for energy, to grow, or to heal.

plain (PLAYN) A large, flat stretch of land.

reservation (reh-zer-VAY-shun) Land that is set aside for Native Americans to live on.

sacred (SAY-kred) Something that is highly respected and considered to be very important.

settler (SET-ul-er) A person who moves to a new land to live.

traditional (truh-DISH-un-ul) Cultural customs that are passed down from parent to child.

Index